Lerner SPORTS

···ESPORTS···
CAREERS

Heather E. Schwartz

Lerner Publications ◆ Minneapolis

SPORTS THRILLS
MEET
RESEARCH SKILLS

Lerner SPORTS

Free Database Trial: **lernersports.com**

Lerner Publications Company
An imprint of Lerner Publishing Group, Inc.
241 First Avenue North
Minneapolis, MN 55401 USA

For reading levels and more information, look up this title at www.lernerbooks.com.

Main body text set in Aptifer Sans LT Pro. Typeface provided by Linotype AG.

Designer: Viet Chu **Photo Editor:** Annie Zheng
Lerner team: Martha Kranes

Library of Congress Cataloging-in-Publication Data

Names: Schwartz, Heather E. author.
Title: Esports careers / by Heather E. Schwartz.
Description: Minneapolis, MN : Lerner Publications, [2024] | Series: Lerner sports. Esports zone | Includes bibliographical references and index. | Audience: Ages 7–11 | Audience: Grades 4–6 | Summary: "More people are watching esports than ever before. But who works in this booming industry? Meet the people who make, play, and report on competitive gaming and learn how they make esports possible"— Provided by publisher.
Identifiers: LCCN 2022049994 (print) | LCCN 2022049995 (ebook) | ISBN 9781728490915 (library binding) | ISBN 9798765602904 (paperback) | ISBN 9781728497389 (ebook)
Subjects: LCSH: eSports (Contests)—Juvenile literature. | Vocational guidance—Juvenile literature. | BISAC: JUVENILE NONFICTION / Careers
Classification: LCC GV1469.34.E86 S349 2024 (print) | LCC GV1469.34.E86 (ebook) | DDC 794.8—dc23/eng/20221018

LC record available at https://lccn.loc.gov/2022049994
LC ebook record available at https://lccn.loc.gov/2022049995

Manufactured in the United States of America
1-53022-51040-2/21/2023

TABLE OF CONTENTS

INTRODUCTION
ESPORTS FOR CHARITY

In 2019, a group of French live streamers hosted a charity event to raise money for vaccines. Over fifty gamers filled the event space and streamed their games to their online followers. Suddenly, gamers in the room went silent as the event host spoke. *Fortnite* streamer Tyler "Ninja" Blevins (*above*) had just given $28,500 to the cause!

Everyone in the room and online began chanting Ninja's name. The event's online chat exploded with emojis. His gift pushed the total raised at the event to $2.9 million. Ninja's gift and the gifts of viewers around the world added up to the largest amount ever given at a charity live stream event. Even France's president, Emmanuel Macron, congratulated the event online.

Streaming is a popular esports career that can bring in a lot of money. But there are many other exciting esports careers too. There's something for everyone who wants to get in the game.

Fast Facts

- In 2022, the global esports industry was valued at more than $1 billion.

- Millions of people around the world watch esports.

- Benedict College in Columbia, South Carolina, became the first historically Black college to offer an esports program.

- St. Mary's University in San Antonio, Texas, hired Texas's first female head coach of a collegiate gaming program.

CHAPTER 1

ESPORTS JOBS IN ACTION

WHEN MOST PEOPLE THINK OF CAREERS IN ESPORTS, THEY THINK ABOUT BECOMING GAMERS. Gamers get to play their favorite video games and build their skills to get better. They can win money at tournaments and maybe even become famous someday.

But gaming isn't the only career for people interested in esports. Would you like to be the star of your own show? Streamers gain fans by posting videos of themselves playing video games. Are you a take-charge type? Esports referees make sure rules are followed and much more.

Esports streamers share their games with online viewers.

Anyone with the right equipment can take part in esports games, but it takes practice to become one of the best.

A lot of people play video games, but how do some people make gaming their job? There are several steps you can take. Most pro gamers start by simply playing games they love. As they play, they work hard to improve their skills through practice and watching others. As they improve, they might start competing in online tournaments.

As gamers rise in the rankings, other esports athletes might ask them to practice and play with a team. But gamers know not to overdo it. They know that screen breaks are good for the body and the brain.

Students can compete in local events near home. Ask a teacher if there is a school esports team you can join. Keep at it, and one day you could join a pro team!

People from around the world travel to watch esports competitions in person.

Gamers who don't join teams have other options. Some gamers build their skills and an audience at the same time through streaming.

Streamers share their games over the internet through platforms such as YouTube and Twitch. Streaming requires a strong internet connection and recording equipment. Streamers often use cameras to show their faces so people can see their reactions to the game.

Streamers use recording programs, cameras, and good lighting to make their videos appealing.

HOW STREAMING PAYS

Famous pro gamers such as Tyler "Ninja" Blevins and Imane "Pokimane" Anys get paid to do what they love in different ways. Viewers can pay to access special streams and chances to win prizes. Ninja and Pokimane also get money from ads on their videos and sponsorship deals with companies.

Imane "Pokimane" Anys is one of the most followed streamers on Twitch.

A referee (*center*) flips a coin before the start of a *League of Legends* event. The team that wins the coin flip will get the first chance to choose a side.

It's not just the visuals that draw in fans. A lot of people want to hear gamers talk, so streamers use mics to record their voices. Most successful streamers are both fun to watch and listen to. They make jokes and share stories.

Like other sports, many pro esports games use referees. A referee makes sure rules are followed. Sometimes they make sure players are using the right equipment. They might also test connections and deal with problems such as broken keyboards.

Esports referees start by learning the rules of games and volunteering at local tournaments. You can practice your referee skills by settling video game arguments at home. Make sure everyone plays fairly and has fun.

Referees test equipment and make sure gamers use approved gear during events.

CHAPTER 2
BEHIND THE SCENES

SOME ESPORTS JOBS HAPPEN BEHIND THE SCENES. If you're great at leading others, you could become a coach. Coaches help players reach their full potential.

Esports coaches organize teams and work closely with players. They help players train and plan ways to win. It's an exciting position for anyone who likes coming up with new plans and ideas. Coaches bring together skilled gamers and help them work together.

Esports coaches need to be leaders who can motivate others. Many people get started by working with friends or amateur teams. Later they might join a pro group.

Esports coaches show players new ways they can improve their games.

COACHING AT THE COLLEGE LEVEL

In 2020, St. Mary's University in San Antonio, Texas, hired Kaitlin Teniente as the head coach for the school's new esports program. She often speaks up to support other female gamers. Teniente is one of the first female head coaches of a college gaming program.

St. Mary's University became the first university in San Antonio to have a varsity-level esports team and a gaming arena.

Game designers can turn their ideas into fun games that millions of people will want to play.

Playing a game you love is fun. Now imagine designing your own game. You could include everything you like about games. The setting, characters, story, and more would be all up to you.

Game designers do that for a living. Some work alone, but most designers work on big teams. Most game designers get a college degree in graphic design, programming, or animation.

Making a video game takes a team of people, including artists, programmers, story writers, and game testers.

You don't have to wait for college to get started. Anyone can create their own games in coding programs such as Scratch. Ask a teacher about ways to learn how to code. As you learn more advanced coding, you can create bigger games.

CHAPTER 3

FINDING AN AUDIENCE

IN 2022, THE GLOBAL ESPORTS INDUSTRY WAS VALUED AT MORE THAN $1 BILLION. Most of the money comes through sponsorships and advertising. The more people watch, the more advertising and sponsorship dollars esports brings in. And a lot of people watch. Around the world, hundreds of millions of people are esports fans.

Fans find out about esports events through the work of marketing and communications teams. They spread the word about tournaments, celebrity events, and everything else happening in esports. They send announcements to the media, write about esports online and in magazines, and write scripts for esports ads. If you have a passion for esports and strong writing skills, a career in marketing and communications could be for you!

Esports marketing teams talk and write about games to attract big audiences.

LEARNING ON THE JOB

Jen Neale works as an esports writer. To learn the job, she worked closely with L.A. Valiant, a pro *Overwatch* team. She went to team practices, watched games, and got to know the players. They taught her all about the game while she got an up-close look at esports.

Thousands of fans attend the biggest esports events.

It takes a lot of work to organize an esports event. Someone has to secure a venue that is big enough to hold everyone. The internet and other gaming tech must be in place. Somebody must be in charge to handle problems, from early planning to the championship match.

ESPORTS FOR EVERYONE

Anna Prosser was Miss Oregon USA in 2011. Her career later turned to esports. She has hosted the Pokémon National and World Championships and other big esports events. She thinks that all kinds of people belong in esports, whether they are gamers or not.

Anna Prosser (*center*) talks about esports on a weekly streaming show.

Esports events managers pull it all together. But that doesn't mean they have to do everything themselves. They're also great at leading others and telling people what needs to be done.

Most events managers have a college degree in business or communications. But if you're interested in managing esports events, you can start by planning parties. You can also run after-school clubs and mentor other students.

Watching esports competitions is exciting. But some games are so fast that people need a little help to understand what's happening on-screen. They need shoutcasters.

Shoutcasters comment on esports events. They watch the game closely, offer play-by-play comments, and raise the excitement. Whether online or in person, shoutcasters are part of the fun in big esports events. They energize the audience and keep them updated at the same time. Sometimes they even interview the players.

Shoutcasters comment on esports events so people watching know what is happening.

Shoutcasters dress up and have fun at a
League of Legends event in 2022.

So how does an esports fan get into shoutcasting? It helps to be an expert in at least one big esports game. Many shoutcasters played esports in college. Some have college degrees in communications or sports management. Learn more by paying attention to shoutcasters when you watch esports. You can practice by watching a recording of a game on YouTube or Twitch and shoutcasting it yourself.

CHAPTER 4

GETTING INTO ESPORTS

IF YOU LOVE GAMING, GETTING INTO ESPORTS MIGHT SEEM EASY. But esports competitions are something new. It can feel scary to join a team or compete against people you don't know.

Clara "Keffals" Sorrenti is a Canadian Twitch streamer and social activist.

Anyone can get involved in esports. You might feel more comfortable if you watch esports pros who have some things in common with you. Women and people of color are getting more involved in gaming. There are plenty of disabled gamers too, such as Keith "Aieron" Knight. LGBTQIA+ streamers such as Clara "Keffals" Sorrenti have also taken the sport by storm.

You can improve your esports skills by taking a leadership role at school. You could organize an esports club, be a team captain, or create flyers to promote your team's events.

Coding is another way to get involved in gaming and esports. Coding can help kids learn about how games work and how to make changes to games.

Learning to code can open many career paths in gaming and beyond.

Many schools teach coding and have competitive coding. Competitive coding combines game design and game play. In *CodeCombat*, players use the coding languages Python, JavaScript, and C++ to advance in the game. The game starts with Ozaria, a program for upper elementary students. As they learn, students level up. They can compete for prizes in the *CodeCombat* AI League.

Colleges around the world offer degrees in programming, animation, and computer graphic design.

LEARNING ABOUT ESPORTS

Benedict College in Columbia, South Carolina, began offering an esports program in 2022. It's the first historically Black college with such a program. Students take classes in communications, writing, and marketing. When they graduate, they're ready for career paths in esports broadcasting, writing, and security.

Are you serious about a career in esports? Some colleges have esports degree programs. If you study esports management, you'll learn about digital marketing and business. Or you might want to study computer science or video game design. Even college programs that don't focus on gaming could help you land a job in esports.

At school, you can join an esports team. Get involved with a coding club. Anything you like to do can help you find your career path. No matter your skills and interests, there's a place for you in esports!

GLOSSARY

AD: short for *advertisement*, a public notice to sell a product or service

AMATEUR: taking part in an activity for fun rather than money

GAMER: a person who regularly plays computer or video games

MENTOR: to teach, advise, or guide someone else

MIC: short for *microphone*, a device that records or amplifies sound by changing it into electricity

PRO: short for *professional*, taking part in an activity to make money

SPONSORSHIP: when a person or a group gives money to someone to promote a product or business

TOURNAMENT: a series of games played to decide a champion

VENUE: the place where an event takes place

LEARN MORE

Gregory, Josh. *Careers in Esports*. Ann Arbor, MI: Cherry Lake, 2020.

Kiddle: Electronic Sports Facts for Kids
https://kids.kiddle.co/Electronic_sports

Miller, Marie-Therese. *Esports Superstars*. Minneapolis: Lerner Publications, 2024.

National Association of Collegiate Esports
https://nacesports.org

National Esports Association
https://nea.gg/students/

Rathburn, Betsy. *Console Gaming*. Minneapolis: Bellwether Media, 2021.

INDEX

PHOTO ACKNOWLEDGMENTS

Image credits: Ethan Miller/Getty Images Sport/Getty Images, p. 4; adamkaz/E+/Getty Images, p. 6; Complexio/E+/Getty Images, p. 7; mikkelwilliam/E+/Getty Images, p. 8; Maskot/DigitalVision/Getty Images, pp. 9, 13; zeljkosantrac/E+/Getty Images, p. 10; Noam Galai/Stringer/Getty Images Entertainment/Getty Images, p. 11; Riot Games/Getty Images, pp. 12, 19, 24; Ann Kosolapova/Shutterstock, p. 14; Joosep Martinson/FIFA/Getty Images, p. 15; DC Studio/Shutterstock, pp. 17, 18; Luis Alvarez/DigitalVision/Getty Images, p. 20; AP Photo/Mark J. Terrill, p. 21; San Francisco Chronicle/Hearst Newspapers/Getty Images, p. 22; Edwin Tan/E+/Getty Images, p. 23; AP Photo/Elaine Thompson, p. 25; The Washington Post/Getty Images, p. 26; alvarez/E+/Getty Images, p. 27; Andia/Universal Images Group/Getty Images, p. 28.
Design elements: sarayut Thaneerat/Moment/Getty Images.
Cover: BJI/Blue Jean Images/Getty Images (bottom); Frame Stock Footage/Shutterstock (top).